To Cyndi -

The path of life is measured by many things - years and friends among them. May you be blessed with the fortune of always having more friends than you number in years!

God's blessings to you always

The Guisings

May 7, 1994

THE WIT AND WISDOM OF
WOMEN

Canadian representatives: General Publishing Co., Ltd., 30 Lesmill Road, Don Mills, Ontario M3B 2T6. International representatives: Worldwide Media Services, Inc., 30 Montgomery Street, Jersey City, New Jersey 07302.

9   8   7   6   5   4   3   2

Digit on the right indicates the number of this printing.

Library of Congress Cataloging-in-Publication Number 93–83456

ISBN 1–56138–302–3

Cover design by Toby Schmidt
Cover illustration by Michael Paraskevas
Interior design by Jacqueline Spadaro
Interior illustration by Steven Nau
Edited by Melissa Stein
Typography by Richard Conklin
Printed in the United States

This book may be ordered by mail from the publisher.
Please add $2.50 for postage and handling.
But try your bookstore first!

Running Press Book Publishers
125 South Twenty-second Street
Philadelphia, Pennsylvania 19103–4399

THE WIT AND WISDOM OF
WOMEN

RUNNING PRESS • PHILADELPHIA, PENNSYLVANIA

Contents

Introduction

The book you hold is a celebration of women's lives, at once funny, poignant, passionate, and irrepressibly joyful. Gathered here are quotes from an astonishing array of women throughout the ages: chefs, homemakers, suffragettes, writers, psychologists, and feminists. No subject is taboo, and each woman speaks freely, from George Sand to George Eliot, from Susan B. Anthony to Hillary Rodham Clinton, from May West to Mae Sarton.

Many of these women, bound by time, place, and circumstance, could not possibly have conversed during their lifetimes—but that doesn't mean we can't delight in a spirited dialogue of our own making. Here you'll find a British aviator clashing with a 19th-century poet, and a former Miss America challenging a Spanish actress. Such differences of opinion enable us to explore the many sides to each issue, but perhaps more revealing are the many areas of accord, where one view illuminates the next. Among these kindred spirits are Emily Dickinson and Alice Walker on the resonance of poetry, Gloria Steinem and Eleanor Roosevelt on self-esteem, and Colette and Cher on the nature of life's mysteries. These unexpected meetings of the mind affirm the universal quality of our experiences.

As you read their words, immerse yourself in the shared wisdom of these extraordinary women—you may discover yourself among them.

Personal Power

I hear the singing of the lives of women,
The clear mystery, the offering and pride.
MURIEL RUKEYSER

Our strength is often composed of the weaknesses we're
damned if we're going to show.
MIGNON MCLAUGHLIN

If the world's a wilderness,
Go, build houses in it!
LUCY LARCOM

. . . women are the architects of society.
HARRIET BEECHER STOWE

We write our own destiny. We become what we do.
MADAME CHIANG KAI-SHEK

A woman is like a tea bag. You never know how strong she is until she gets into hot water.
ELEANOR ROOSEVELT

Considering how dangerous everything is nothing is frightening.

GERTRUDE STEIN

I have a lot of things to prove to myself. One is that I can live my life fearlessly.

OPRAH WINFREY

Nothing and everything cannot coexist. To believe in one is to deny the other. Fear is really nothing and love is everything. Whenever light enters darkness, the darkness is abolished.

HELEN SCHUCMAN

Our way is not soft grass, it's a mountain path with lots of rocks. But it goes upwards, forward, toward the sun.

RUTH WESTHEIMER

Women are always being tested . . . but ultimately, each of us has to define who we are individually and then do the very best job we can to grow into that.

HILLARY RODHAM CLINTON

If you think you're too small to have an impact, try going to bed with a mosquito.

ANITA KODDICK

. . . some of us just go along . . . until that marvelous day people stop intimidating us—or should I say we refuse to let them intimidate us?

PEGGY LEE

If you give in to intimidation, you'll go on being intimidated.

AUNG SAN SUU KYI

. . . I'm not going to lie down and let trouble walk over me.

ELLEN GLASGOW

I don't want to be a passenger in my own life.

DIANE ACKERMAN

I will not be just a tourist in the world of images, just watching images passing by which I cannot live in, make love to, possess as permanent sources of joy and ecstasy.

ANAÏS NIN

You are the architect of your personal experience.

SHIRLEY MACLAINE

A grown woman did not need safety or its dreams. She was the safety she longed for.

TONI MORRISON

As I started looking, I found more and more.

VALERIE STEELE

14

The true exercise of freedom is—cannily and wisely and with grace—to move inside what space confines—and not seek to know what lies beyond and cannot be touched or tasted.

A. S. BYATT

Should-haves solve nothing. It's the next thing to happen that needs thinking about.

ALEXANDRA RIPLEY

Liberation means that I am confident enough of myself that I can give it to others, and love means that I am confident enough about that other that I can trust him with my gift.

CAROL TRAVIS

Power is the ability to do good things for others.

BROOKE ASTOR

Asserting yourself while respecting others is a very good way to win respect yourself.

JANICE LAROUCHE

The woman who has sprung free has emotional mobility. She is able to move toward the things that are satisfying to her and away from those that are not. She is free, also, to succeed.

COLETTE DOWLING

. . . as one goes through life one learns that if you don't paddle your own canoe, you don't move.

KATHARINE HEPBURN

Women . . . often . . . need to return to their past, to the women who were part of that past, to girlhood when a self existed that was individual and singular, defined neither by men, nor children, nor home, almost as though with the layers of roles and responsibilities they have covered over a real person and must now peel back those layers and reclaim the self that was just emerging in adolescence.

MARY HELEN WASHINGTON

Peace means loyalty to self. . . . And loyalty to one's self means never a gap between thought, speech, act.

RUTH BEEBE HILL

. . . one of the goals of life is to try and be in touch with one's most personal themes—the values, ideas, styles, colors that are the touchstones of one's own individual life, its real texture and substance.

GLORIA VANDERBILT

Strategies

My motto—*sans limites.*
ISADORA DUNCAN

What you can't get out of, get into wholeheartedly.
MIGNON McLAUGHLIN

If you can't change your fate, change your attitude.
AMY TAN

It's no laughing matter, but it doesn't matter if you laugh.

JENNIE GUDMUNDSEN

You live. No use asking whether life will bring you pleasure or unhappiness, whether it will prove a blessing or a curse. Who could answer these questions? You live, you breathe.

GEORGE SAND

I used to trouble about what life was for—now being alive seems sufficient reason.

JOANNA FIELD

Surviving meant being born over and over.

ERICA JONG

The trick to life, I can say now in my advanced age, is to stop trying to make it so important.

LORETTA YOUNG

The more passions and desires one has, the more ways one has of being happy.

CHARLOTTE–CATHERINE

I'm afraid I'm an incorrigible life-lover, life-wonderer, and adventurer.

EDITH WHARTON

I'm the foe of moderation, the champion of excess. If I may lift a line from a die-hard whose identity is lost in the shuffle, "I'd rather be strongly wrong than weakly right."

TALLULAH BANKHEAD

In order to live . . . act; in order to act . . . make choices. . .

AYN RAND

All the great decisions in my life have been made in less than half an hour.

CARMEN MAURA

Life is something to do when you can't get to sleep.

FRAN LEBOWITZ

We cannot take anything for granted, beyond the first mathematical formula. Question everything else.

MARIA MITCHELL

If you want to live on the edge of life, you need to be flexible.

KIM NOVAK

I like walking the edge between soft and sharp, tough and fragile.

MIGNON FAGET

. . . there is a luxury in being quiet in the heart of chaos.

VIRGINIA WOOLF

I praise loudly; I blame softly.

CATHERINE II

. . . what matters most is that we learn from living.

DORIS LESSING

Where I was born and where and how I have lived is unimportant. It is what I have done with where I have been that should be of interest.

GEORGIA O'KEEFFE

Doing the best at this moment puts you in the best place for the next moment.

OPRAH WINFREY

. . . life can only be kept by giving it away. But then it will bloom.

ANNE RIVERS SIDDONS

25

Self-Respect

Self-confidence: When you think that your greatest fault is being too hard on yourself.

JUDITH VIORST

. . . self-esteem isn't everything; it's just that there's nothing without it.

GLORIA STEINEM

27

. . . self-regard is the root of regard for one's fellows.

MARGARET THATCHER

It is not easy to be sure that being yourself is worth the trouble, but [we do know] it is our sacred duty.

FLORIDA SCOTT–MAXWELL

We inhabit ourselves without valuing ourselves, unable to see that here, now, this very moment is sacred; but once it's gone—its value is incontestable.

JOYCE CAROL OATES

To be a leader you must feel that you are both every-thing and nothing—nothing in that you are on this earth for a few years out of billions . . . everything, because you are at the center of all activity in your world.

EDITH WEINER

Follow your image as far as you can no matter how useless you think it is. Push yourself.

NIKKI GIOVANNI

Would that there were an award for people who come to understand the concept of enough. Good enough. Successful enough. Thin enough. Rich enough. Socially responsible enough. When you have self-respect you have enough, and when you have enough, you have self-respect.

GAIL SHEEHY

We have only one real shot at liberation, and that is to emancipate ourselves from within.

COLETTE DOWLING

To find in ourselves what makes life worth living is risky business, for it means that once we know we must seek it. It also means that without it life will be valueless.

MARSHA SINETAR

PEARL S. BUCK

Ambition

All things are possible until they are proved impossible—
and even the impossible may only be so, as of now.
PEARL S. BUCK

I've always tried to go a step past wherever people
expected me to end up.
BEVERLY SILLS

After the feet of beauty fly my own.
EDNA ST. VINCENT MILLAY

Nothing that is beautiful is easy, but everything is possible.
MERCEDES DE ACOSTA

It's hard to stay committed . . . to stay in touch with the goal without saying there's something wrong with myself, my goal, the world.
NANCY HOGSHEAD

We don't know who we are until we see what we can do.
MARTHA GRIMES

I wonder if we climb to heaven over the ruins of many cherished schemes.
LAUREL LEE

Saddle your dreams afore you ride 'em.
MARY WEBB

Nothing is so inexorable as a promise to your pride.
BERYL MARKHAM

. . . in dreams begins responsibility.
EDNA O'BRIEN

. . . I can do what I want to do and that has been my greatest gift.

FAITH RINGGOLD

The excitement, the true excitement, was always in starting again. Nothing's worse than an accomplished task, a realized dream.

MARILYN HARRIS

Reality was much prettier than a dream.

CAROLINA MARIA DE JESUS

Work

Work is love made visible.
AMA ATA AIDOO

The days you work are the best days.
GEORGIA O'KEEFFE

I knew early on that I'd have to work, work, work if I wanted to amount to much; plums don't drop into plain girls' laps.
GLENDA JACKSON

The mix of our ambitions and our cleverness—the ability to piece together work that will both satisfy and support us—is the secret to surviving, even thriving.
WENDY REID CRISP

The vital, successful people I have met all had one common characteristic. They had a plan.
MARILYN VAN DERBUR

I got myself a start by giving myself a start.
MADAM C. J. WALKER

This became a credo of mine . . . attempt the impossible in order to improve your work.

BETTE DAVIS

Find something you're passionate about and keep tremendously interested in it.

JULIA CHILD

Find out what you like doing best and get someone to pay you for doing it.

KATHERINE WHITEHORN

It is not true that there is dignity in all work. Some jobs are definitely better than others.
FRAN LEBOWITZ

Without discipline, there's no life at all.
KATHARINE HEPBURN

Without work I am nothing.
WINIFRED HOLTBY

When you cease to make a contribution, you begin to die.

ELEANOR ROOSEVELT

The secret of joy in work is contained in one word—excellence. To know how to do something well is to enjoy it.

PEARL S. BUCK

Genius is immediate, but talent takes time.

JANET FLANNER

GERTRUDE STEIN

Success

We see achievement as purposeful and monolithic, like the sculpting of a massive tree trunk that has first to be brought from the forest and then shaped by long labor to assert the artist's vision, rather than something crafted from odds and ends, like a patchwork quilt, and lovingly used to warm different nights and bodies.

MARY CATHERINE BATESON

None of us suddenly becomes something overnight. The preparations have been in the making for a lifetime.

GAIL GODWIN

Life is not orderly. No matter how we try to make life so, right in the middle of it we die, lose a leg, fall in love, drop a jar of applesauce.

NATALIE GOLDBERG

Hardships and handicaps can . . . stimulate our energy to survive them. You'll find if you study the lives of people who've accomplished things, it's often been done with the help of great willpower in overcoming this and that.

BEATRICE WOOD

Even the most fortunate have a lot of crumpled rose leaves under their forty mattresses of ease.

DOROTHY DIX

Show me a person who has never made a mistake and I'll show you somebody who has never achieved much.

JOAN COLLINS

. . . this thing that we call "failure" is not the falling down, but the staying down.

MARY PICKFORD

It is better to be young in your failures than old in your successes.

FLANNERY O'CONNOR

In order to succeed, at times you have to make something from nothing.

RUTH MICKLEBY–LAND

Everybody knows if you are too careful you are so occupied in being careful that you are sure to stumble over something.

GERTRUDE STEIN

Tragedy happens only when you are trying to live well.

MARTHA NUSSBAUM

Pride . . . can never achieve so much as love, because it can never face the extremes of nobility and debasement which love can face and which are our life.

STEVIE SMITH

At the root of human responsibility is the concept of perfection, the urge to achieve it, the intelligence to find a path towards it, and the will to follow that path, if not to the end at least the distance needed to rise above individual limitations and environmental impediments.

AUNG SAN SUU KYI

Nothing liberates our greatness like the desire to help, the desire to serve.

MARIANNE WILLIAMSON

Accomplishments have no color.

LEONTYNE PRICE

The wonder is what you can make a paradise out of.

EVA HOFFMAN

Most of us live our lives devoid of cinematic moments.
NORA EPHRON

He has achieved success who has lived well, laughed
often, and loved much . . . who has filled his niche and
accomplished his task; who has left the world better than
he found it, whether an improved poppy, a perfect poem,
or a rescued soul. . . .
BESSIE ANDERSON STANLEY

Sooner or later we all discover that the important
moments in life are not the advertised ones, not the
birthdays, the graduations, the weddings, not the great
goals achieved. The real milestones are less prepossessing.
They come to the door of memory unannounced, stray
dogs that amble in, sniff around a bit, and simply never
leave. Our lives are measured by these.
SUSAN B. ANTHONY

Women have to summon up courage to fulfill dormant dreams.

ALICE WALKER

There is no point at which you can say, "Well, I'm successful now. I might as well take a nap."

CARRIE FISHER

Connecting

. . . where does one person end and another person begin?

IRIS MURDOCH

I believe that basically people are people . . . but it is our differences which charm, delight and frighten us.

AGNES NEWTON KEITH

We're frightened of what makes us different.

ANNE RICE

Differences are sources of strength for each of us—so long as they are not used against us.

JEAN BAKER MILLER

What is exciting is not for one person to be stronger than the other . . . but for two people to have met their match and yet they are equally as stubborn, as obstinate, as passionate, as crazy as the other.

BARBRA STREISAND

What loneliness is more lonely than distrust?
GEORGE ELIOT

The biggest mistake is believing there is one right way to listen, to talk, to have a conversation—or a relationship.
DEBORAH TANNEN

The intimacy that exists between men and women can seem the confrontation between good and evil, the place where there is the greatest chance of their being resolved by compassion and insight. It is here that souls are bared. Here in the welter of complete exposure we meet our glories and our sins, and we can see when we should have accused ourselves not the other: here too we may find the mutual support to enable us to say, "I see myself."
FLORIDA SCOTT–MAXWELL

Men have skin, but women have flesh—flesh that takes and gives light.

NATALIE BARNEY

. . . women forget all those things they don't want to remember, and remember everything they don't want to forget. . . . Then they act and do things accordingly.

ZORA NEALE HURSTON

Carve not upon a stone when I am dead
     The praise which remorseful mourners give
To women's graves—a tardy recompense—
     But speak them while I live.

ELIZABETH AKERS ALLEN

It's entirely in your power to regulate the degree to which you peel back the layers of your personality when you disclose yourself to someone. You can keep that person on the surface, or you can allow her to penetrate, by degrees or directly, to the core.

HARRIET BRAIKER

The more you try to be interested in other people, the more you find out about yourself.

THEA ASTLEY

Television has proved that people will look at anything rather than each other.

ANN LANDERS

How did a person survive without intimacy? Didn't you need at least one person in the world to know who you really were?

JUDITH FREEMAN

The flip side to being attracted to unavailable people is how bored you are by available people. Available people are terrifying because they want to hang around long enough to know you, to like you, to accept you. The problem is not that you attract unavailable people—the problem is that you give them your number.

MARIANNE WILLIAMSON

. . . a garden dies quickly without a loving gardener to keep it alive.

MAY SARTON

Paradoxical though it may sound: whenever one tries too desperately to be physically close to some beloved person, whenever one throws all one has into one's longing for that person, one is really giving him short change. For one has no reserves left then for a true encounter.

ETTY HILLESUM

I made you take time to look at what I saw and when you took time to really notice my flower you hung all your associations with flowers on my flower and you write about my flower as if I think and see what you think and see—and I don't.

GEORGIA O'KEEFFE

Friendship

Sincerity is as valuable as radium.
FANNIE FLAGG

It's funny how your initial approach to a person can determine your feelings toward them, no matter what facts develop later on.
DOROTHY UHNAK

57

They *are* love, those rare, binding early friendships. Not everyone has them, and almost no one gets more than one. The others, the later ones, are not the same. These grow in a soil found only in the country of the young, and are possible only there, because their medium is unbroken time and proximity and discovery, and later there is not enough of any of those for the total, ongoing immersions that these friendships are.

ANNE RIVERS SIDDONS

We all live on bases of shifting sands, [and] need trust.

ERMA J. FISK

Reinforce the stitch that ties us, and I will do the same for you.

DORIS SCHWERIN

When friends ask for a second cup they are open to conversation . . .

GAIL PARENT

Sometimes, with luck, we find the kind of true friend, male or female, that appears only two or three times in a lucky lifetime, one that will winter us and summer us, grieve, rejoice, and travel with us.

BARBARA HOLLAND

Oh, the comfort, the inexpressible comfort of feeling safe with a person, having neither to weigh thoughts nor measure words, but pouring them all right out, just as they are, chaff and grain together; certain that a faithful hand will take and sift them, keep what is worth keeping, and then with the breath of kindness throw the rest away.

DINAH MARIA MULOCK CRAIK

. . . I feel what I can only call a molecular lushness close to my face: the deep powder of friendship.

GRETEL EHRLICH

Familiarity breeds content.

ANNA QUINDLEN

One can never pay in gratitude; one can only pay "in kind" somewhere else in life. . . .

ANNE MORROW LINDBERGH

. . . the ones that give, get back in kind.

PAM DURBAN

We must treat all people as if they were at least better than ourselves.

SAINT TERESA

Those who have suffered understand suffering and therefore extend their hand.

PATTI SMITH

Being considerate of others will take you and your children further in life than any college or professional degree.

MARIAN WRIGHT EDELMAN

The growth of true friendship may be a lifelong affair.

SARAH ORNE JEWETT

I can trust my friends. . . . These people force me to examine myself, encourage me to grow.

CHER

When someone tells you the truth, lets you think for yourself, experience your own emotions, he is treating you as a true equal. As a friend.

WHITNEY OTTO

A faithful friend is a strong defense;
And he that hath found him hath found a treasure.

LOUISA MAY ALCOTT

Style

The only real elegance is in the mind. If you've got that, the rest follows from it.

DIANA VREELAND

Tenderness is the grace of the heart, as style is the grace of the mind. . . .

MAY SARTON

It's all right for a perfect stranger to kiss your hand as long as he's perfect.
MAE WEST

He is every other inch a gentleman.
DAME REBECCA WEST

A lady is one who never shows her underwear unintentionally.
LILLIAN DAY

A courteous person will always make everyone around him feel at his best and most alive. No matter how superior his knowledge, his breeding and so on, he will bring to his meeting with another person an absolutely genuine interest, respect and concern for that person; and above all, he will give him his whole *attention* without curiosity or demand, and so immediately communicate to the other a freedom and sureness of which, perhaps, he did not know himself to be capable. . . .

HELEN M. LUKE

The dying process begins the minute we are born, but it accelerates during dinner parties.

CAROL MATTHAU

At times . . . one is downright thankful for the self-absorption of other people.

GAIL GODWIN

The way you say a thing is part of what you say, so you have to choose the right way.

ISABEL BISHOP

. . . the whole art of life is knowing the right time to say things.

MAEVE BINCHY

Blessed is the man who, having nothing to say, abstains from giving in words evidence of the fact.

GEORGE ELIOT

Desire

In love there are two things: bodies and words.
JOYCE CAROL OATES

Bodies cannot lie.
AGNES DE MILLE

What you think is the heart may well be another organ.
JEANETTE WINTERSON

My mind and body are going in the same direction
but not at the same speed.
MARGARET RANDALL

So subtly is the fume of life designed
To clarify the pulse and cloud the mind.
EDNA ST. VINCENT MILLAY

Passionate love dissolved like summer snow.
MAY SARTON

Desire disappears in its fulfillment, which is cold comfort
for hot blood. . .
ANGELA CARTER

What is beyond Desire, but Desire?
GRETEL EHRLICH

If somebody makes me laugh, I'm his slave for life.
BETTE MIDLER

. . . wit . . . is, after all, a form of arousal. We challenge one another to be funnier and smarter. It's high-energy play. It's the way friends make love to one another.
ANNE GOTTLIEB

From the moment I was six I felt sexy. And let me tell you it was hell, sheer hell, waiting to do something about it.
BETTE DAVIS

Sex is an emotion in motion. . . . Love is what you make it and who you make it with.
MAE WEST

All my lovers have been geniuses; it's the one thing on which I insist.

ISADORA DUNCAN

. . . . the life and love of the body is a noble thing, against which the intellect and the spirit need not wage war.

MICHELE ROBERTS

The flesh is suffused by the spirit, and it is forgetting this in the act of love-making that creates cynicism and despair.

MAY SARTON

Sex is perhaps like culture—a luxury that only becomes an art after generations of leisurely acquaintance.

ALICE B. TOKLAS

Sexual Politics

Women have to be twice as good to get half as far as men.

AGNES MACPHAIL

When women go wrong, men go right after them.

MAE WEST

Don't accept rides from strange men—and remember that all men are as strange as hell.
Robin Morgan

I am a woman meant for a man, but I never found a man who could compete.
Bette Davis

A desire to have all of the fun is nine-tenths of the law of chivalry.
Dorothy Leigh Sayers

I married beneath me—all women do.
Nancy Astor

The witty woman especially is a tragic figure in America. Wit destroys eroticism and eroticism destroys wit, so a woman must choose between taking lovers and taking no prisoners.

FLORENCE KING

I fear nothing so much as a man who is witty all day long.

MADAME DE SÉVIGNÉ

. . . friendship has too much resembled for men the camaraderie of battle, for women the consolations of passivity; marriage has owed too much to romance, too little to friendship.

CAROLYN G. HEILBRUN

It's only when we have nothing else to hold onto that we're willing to try something very audacious and scary; only when we're free of the allure, the enticements, the familiar and comfortable lies of the patriarchy will we be able to alter our perspective enough, change our feelings enough, gather enough courage to see and grab the next rope and continue our journey home.

SONIA JOHNSON

Long ago I understood that it wasn't merely my being a woman that was preventing my being welcomed into the world of what I long thought of as my peers. It was that I had succeeded in an undertaking few men have even attempted: I have become myself.

ALICE KOLLER

The word "feminist" is now used most often to divide women from their own interests and worse, against one another.

SUZY MCKEE CHARNAS

74

. . . the Golden Rule works for men as written, but for women it should go the other way around. We need to do unto ourselves as we do unto others.

GLORIA STEINEM

In a society where the rights and potential of women are constrained, no man can be truly free. He may have power, but he will not have freedom.

MARY ROBINSON

"Polly Cook did it and she hated every stitch she did in it."

SAMPLER, 18TH CENTURY

. . . what women want is what men want. They want respect.

MARILYN VOS SAVANT

Love

If you give your life as a wholehearted response to love, then love will wholeheartedly respond to you.

MARIANNE WILLIAMSON

We discovered in each other and ourselves worlds, galaxies, a universe.

ANNE RIVERS SIDDONS

... What I do
And what I dream include thee, as the wine
Must taste of its own grapes.
ELIZABETH BARRETT BROWNING

It was enough just to sit there without words.
LOUISE ERDRICH

The beginning is giving. . .
MURIEL RUKEYSER

From the beginning women understand devotion, it is a natural grace with them; they have only to learn where to direct it.
WILLA CATHER

Love has nothing to do with what you are expecting to get—only with what you are expecting to give—which is everything.

KATHARINE HEPBURN

. . . a relationship has a momentum, it must change and develop, and will tend to move toward the point of greatest commitment.

CAROLYN G. HEILBRUN

Love is or it ain't. Thin love ain't love at all.

TONI MORRISON

Don't be afraid to feel as angry or as loving as you can.

LENA HORNE

Love knows no honor; people in love do things that they never thought they'd do and that they've always despised other people for doing. They violate not only their own scruples but their own *style*.

PAULINE KAEL

. . . We didn't choose our jealousies,
dealt us like a hand we'll never play exactly right.

CHRISTIANE JACOX KYLE

If your head tells you one thing and your heart tells you another, before you do anything, you should first decide whether you have a better head or a better heart.

MARILYN VOS SAVANT

There are no events but thoughts and the heart's hard turning, the heart's slow learning where to love and whom. The rest is merely gossip, and tales for other times.

ANNIE DILLARD

Nothing matters but [love]. It demolishes the days and happily turns them into passageways.

GRETEL EHRLICH

An obvious obsession would have been easier. To talk about him ceaselessly while alone and introduce him into every conversation. But thinking about him is even too dangerous. Sleep in the ordinary way impossible because he intrudes. . . .

CAROLE MORIN

Fancy lovers never last.

MAXINE HONG KINGSTON

If you have once been deeply in love with someone, you never lose him or her. You can invoke that person's presence by just thinking about him.

ELEANOR LAMBERT

People come and go in life, but they never leave your dreams. Once they're in your subconscious, they are immortal.

PATRICIA HAMPL

You know, a heart can be broken, but it keeps on beating, just the same.

FANNIE FLAGG

Forgiveness is an act of the will, and the will can function regardless of the temperature of the heart.

CORRIE TEN BOOM

Forgiveness is the key to action and freedom.

HANNAH ARENDT

So sad! That is the saddest part when you lose someone you love—that person keeps changing. And later you wonder, Is this the same person I lost? Maybe you lost more, maybe less, ten thousand different things that come from your memory or imagination—and you do not know which is which, which was true, which is false.

AMY TAN

The loss of young first love is so painful that it borders on the ludicrous.

MAYA ANGELOU

Whoever it is you fall in love with for the first time, not just love but be in love with, is the one who will always make you angry, the one you can't be logical about. It may be that you are settled in another place, it may be that you are happy, but the one who took your heart wields final power.

JEANETTE WINTERSON

We can perhaps learn to prepare for love. We can welcome its coming, we can learn to treasure and cherish it when it comes, but we cannot make it happen. We are elected into love.

IRENE CLAREMONT DE CASTILLEJO

[Nothing] . . . leads to love. It is love who throws himself across your path. And then he either blocks it for ever or, if he abandons it, leaves it in rack and ruin.

COLETTE

I wonder why love is so often equated with joy when it is everything else as well. Devastation, balm, obsession, granting and receiving excessive value, and losing it again. It is recognition, often of what you are not but might be. It sears and it heals. It is beyond pity and above law. It can seem like truth. But what is truth?

FLORIDA SCOTT–MAXWELL

Work is what gives us our bread and butter, stability and place in the world, but love keeps us human. Any old kind of love.

BARBARA HOLLAND

It is a curious thought, but it is only when you see people looking ridiculous, that you realize just how much you love them.

AGATHA CHRISTIE

Love is like playing checkers. You have to know which man to move.

JACKIE "MOMS" MABLEY

A man's kiss is his signature.

MAE WEST

Love comes gradually with our worry, relief, and care—with what we have invested of ourselves.

FRANCES KARLEN SANTAMARIA

Love is the extremely difficult realization that something other than oneself is real.

IRIS MURDOCH

I'm convinced that it's energy and humor. The two of them combined equal charm.

JUDITH KRANTZ

Love, the quest; marriage, the conquest; divorce, the inquest.

HELEN ROWLAND

Love is that vital essence that pervades and permeates, from the center to the circumference, the graduating circles of all thought and action. Love is the talisman of human weal and woe—the open sesame to every soul.

ELIZABETH CADY STANTON

Love is not self-sacrifice, but the most profound assertion of your own needs and values. It is for your *own* happiness that you need the person you love, and that is the greatest compliment, the greatest tribute you can pay to that person.

AYN RAND

Love is indeed not a state that we are "in" or "out" of. It comes as a gift when we risk ourselves, our *whole* selves. . . .

PENELOPE WASHBOURN

We are told that people stay in love because of chemistry, or because they remain intrigued with each other, because of many kindnesses, because of luck. . . . But part of it has got to be forgiveness and gratefulness. The understanding that, so, you're no bargain, but you love and you are loved. Anyway.

ELLEN GOODMAN

Marriage

They err, who say that husbands can't be lovers.
ANNE FINCH

A successful marriage requires falling in love many times, always with the same person.
MIGNON MCLAUGHLIN

Opposites attract, but like is much easier to be married to.
DIANA DOUGLAS DARRID

The real marriage of true minds is for any two people to possess a sense of humour or irony pitched in exactly the same key, so that their joint glances at any subject cross like interarching searchlights.

EDITH WHARTON

Marriages, like careers, need constant nurturing. . . . the secret of having it all is loving it all.

JOYCE BROTHERS

Like species, couples die out or evolve.

MARGE PIERCY

. . . the more time you invest in a marriage, the more valuable it becomes.

AMY GRANT

After a few years of marriage a man can look right at a woman without seeing her and a woman can see right through a man without looking at him.

HELEN ROWLAND

A man in love is incomplete until he is married. Then he's finished.

ZSA ZSA GABOR

We all have a childhood dream that when there is love, everything goes like silk, but the reality is that marriage requires a lot of compromise.

RAQUEL WELCH

A married couple is a dangerous machine!

IRIS MURDOCH

Solitude

It's like magic. When you live by yourself, all your annoying habits are gone!
MERRILL MARKOE

When I'm alone, I can sleep crossways in bed without an argument.
ZSA ZSA GABOR

I love being single. It's almost like being rich.

SUE GRAFTON

Single life should be experimental in nature and open to accidents. Some accidents are happy ones.

BARBARA HOLLAND

Certain springs are tapped only when we are alone. . . . women need solitude in order to find again the true essence of themselves; that firm strand which will be the indispensable center of a whole web of human relationships.

ANNE MORROW LINDBERGH

Wouldn't it be nice if everybody understood without being told that you need a certain amount of space?

MARY HIGGINS CLARK

Incessant company is as bad as solitary confinement.
VIRGINIA WOOLF

Once you have lived with another, it is a great torture to have to live alone.
CARSON MCCULLERS

Surely even those immune from the world . . . need the touch of another . . .
EUDORA WELTY

Sometimes it is less hard to wake up feeling lonely when you are alone than wake up feeling lonely when you are with someone.
LIV ULLMANN

. . . there are days when solitude . . . is a heady wine which intoxicates you with freedom, others when it is a bitter tonic, and still others when it is a poison which makes you beat your head against the wall.

COLETTE

When we cannot bear to be alone, it means we do not properly value or appreciate the only companion we will have from birth to death—ourselves.

EDA LESHAN

Being solitary is being alone well: being alone luxuriously immersed in doings of your own choice, aware of the fullness of your own presence rather than of the absence of others. Because solitude is an achievement.

ALICE KOLLER

Mothering

Children reinvent your world for you.
SUSAN SARANDON

Sometimes the strength of motherhood is greater than natural laws.
BARBARA KINGSOLVER

The biggest surprise, which is also the best, is that I didn't know I would love motherhood as much as I do.
DEBORAH NORVILLE

It's good for a child to lose as well as win. They must learn in life they are going to be up today and maybe down tomorrow.

RUBY MIDDLETON FORSYTHE

Being a mother is my most important role in life.

THERESA RUSSELL

I know why families were created, with all their imperfections. They humanize you. They are made to make you forget yourself occasionally, so that the beautiful balance of life is not destroyed.

ANAÏS NIN

To me, life is tough enough without having someone
kick you from the inside.

RITA RUDNER

Your mother loves you like the deuce while you are
coming. Wrapped up there under her heart is perhaps
the cosiest time in existence. Then she and you are one,
companions.

EMILY CARR

I had forgotten how sensuous babies are—all skin and
touch and need—and how central to their care is one's
own sensuality.

ANNE TRUITT

Babies don't come with directions on the back or batteries that can be removed. Motherhood is twenty-four hours a day, seven days a week. You can't "leave the office."

PAT SCHROEDER

Childhood's learning is made up of moments. It isn't steady: It's a pulse.

EUDORA WELTY

We must learn the loving of a first child step by step, as we learn to sustain love in marriage. The loving of a first baby is like an acquired gift, or skill. The second child, I imagine, comes into that love ready-made.

FRANCES KARLEN SANTAMARIA

Nothing is more dependable than a child's digestive juices.

RENEE HAWKLEY

To talk to a child, to fascinate him, is much more difficult than to win an electoral victory. But it is also more rewarding.

COLETTE

When the strongest words for what I have to offer come out of me sounding like words I remember from my mother's mouth, then I either have to reassess the meaning of everything I have to say now, or re-examine the worth of her old words.

AUDRE LORDE

In the beginning there was my mother. A shape. A shape and a force, standing in the light. You could see her energy; it was visible in the air. Against any background she stood out. . . .
MARILYN KRYSL

My mother is my mirror and I am hers.
What do we see? Our face grown young again . . .
MARGE PIERCY

Adults look at their parents as people with histories and complexities and, often, mysteries that will never be fully unraveled.
PATTI DAVIS

If we can genuinely honor our mother and father we are not only at peace with ourselves but we can then give birth to our future.
SHIRLEY MacLAINE

A daughter is a woman that cares about where she came from and takes care of them that took care of her.

Toni Morrison

The relationship between a mother and her daughter is as varied, as mysterious, as constantly changing and inter-connected as the patterns that touch, move away from, and touch again in a kaleidoscope.

Lyn Lifshin

You never *will* finish being a daughter. . . . You will be one when you're ninety and so will I.

Gail Godwin

. . . I love my daughter. She and I have shared my body. There is a part of her mind that is a part of mine. But when she was born, she sprang from me like a slippery fish, and has been swimming away ever since.

Amy Tan

No people are ever as divided as those of the same blood.

MAVIS GALLANT

If you can't hold them in your arms, please hold them in your heart.

LORRAINE HALE

It is not until you become a mother that your judgement slowly turns to compassion and understanding.

ERMA BOMBECK

She never quite leaves her children at home, even when she doesn't take them along.

MARGARET CULKIN BANNING

We don't have to achieve to be accepted by our families. We just have to be. Our membership is not based on credentials but on birth.

ELLEN GOODMAN

Grown don't mean nothing to a mother. A child is a child. They get bigger, older, but grown? What's that supposed to mean? In my heart it don't mean a thing.

TONI MORRISON

The trouble with looking back is that we can't change the past. We can, hopefully, talk honestly and openly with our adult children, and even make amends—but the place where we really have a second chance is with our grandchildren.

EDA LESHAN

105

A mother becomes a true grandmother the day she stops noticing the terrible things her children do because she is so enchanted with the wonderful things her grandchildren do.

LOIS WYSE

One didn't issue instructions to comets. Grown children did what they had to do, and parents could only grit their teeth and watch and pray for them to get through it.

LISA ALTHER

No matter how old a mother is she watches her middle-aged children for signs of improvement.

FLORIDA SCOTT-MAXWELL

Childhood

One of the luckiest things that can happen to you in life is . . . to have a happy childhood.
AGATHA CHRISTIE

What we remember from childhood we remember forever—permanent ghosts, stamped, imprinted, eternally seen.
CYNTHIA OZICK

Little girls are cute and small only to adults. To one another they are not cute. They are life-sized.
MARGARET ATWOOD

Few, if any, survive their teens. Most surrender to the vague but murderous pressure of adult conformity.

MAYA ANGELOU

Sometimes when I come across an old photograph of myself, particularly one of those taken when I was ten or twelve or thereabouts, I stare at it for a while trying to locate the person I was then, among all the persons I've been, trying to see stretched out down the years the magnetic chain linking the onlooker and the looked at, the gay expectant child and the sober near-adult.

JOAN FRANCES BENNETT

I had the total attention of both my parents, and was secure in the knowledge of being loved. . . . My memories of falling asleep at night are to the comfortable sound of my parents' voices, voices which conveyed in their tones the message that these two people loved and trusted one another.

JILL KER CONWAY

Setting out in this world, a child feels so indelible. He only comes to find out later that it's all the others along his way who are making themselves indelible to him.

EUDORA WELTY

What we forget as children is that our parents are children, also. The child in them has not been satisfied or met or loved, often. Not always, but very often. Oftener, actually, than is admitted.

EDNA O'BRIEN

. . . when pain has been intertwined with love and closeness, it's very difficult to believe that love and closeness can be experienced without pain.

GLORIA STEINEM

Love is the most important ingredient in living, children are our greatest treasure, all human beings all over the world need and deserve the same opportunities for the fullest use of their abilities, and this planet, the only one we know, must be treasured and not defiled.

EDA LeSHAN

We need to take care of ourselves, our relationships, and reinforce our connection to the world.
MELODY BEATTIE

Feeling gratitude isn't born in us—it's something we are taught, and in turn, we teach our children.
JOYCE BROTHERS

When you realize the value of all life, you dwell less on what is past and concentrate more on the preservation of the future.
DIAN FOSSEY

The trick for grown-ups is to make the effort to recapture what we knew automatically as children.
CAROL LAWRENCE

Growth

. . . one changes from day to day . . . every few years one becomes a new being.

GEORGE SAND

Our consciousness rarely registers the beginning of a growth within us any more than without us: there have been many circulations of the sap before we detect the smallest sign of the bud.

GEORGE ELIOT

. . . time is compressed like the fist I close on my knee. . . . I hold inside it the clues and solutions and the power for what I must do now.

MARGARET ATWOOD

There is no beyond, there is only here, the infinitely small, infinitely great and utterly demanding present.

IRIS MURDOCH

If we don't change, we don't grow. If we don't grow, we are not really living.

GAIL SHEEHY

There is no good reason why we should not develop and change until the last day we live.

KAREN HORNEY

I avoid looking forward or backward, and try to keep looking upward.

CHARLOTTE BRONTË

. . . some things are never completed; you just leave off.

BARBARA GUEST

The one thing I've learned in this business—and in this life—is: whenever you say, nothing is going to happen—something happens.

MARGARET WHITING

Things do change—if you let them.

PATRICIA MACLACHLAN

Life is a movable feast . . . a tour in a post chaise, but who's to be considered as moving, it or you? The answer is—quick over the abyss, and be damned to being. Start *doing*.

HORTENSE CALISHER

People create their own questions because they're afraid to look straight. All you have to do is look straight and see the road, and when you see it, don't sit looking at it—walk.

AYN RAND

Remember if people talk behind your back, it only means you are two steps ahead!

FANNIE FLAGG

Is this not where life's possibilities lie? Not necessarily to arrive, but *always* to be on the *way*, in *movement*.

LIV ULLMANN

You should always know when you're shifting gears in life. You should leave your era—it should never leave you.

LEONTYNE PRICE

He who hesitates is a damn fool.

MAE WEST

Of any stopping place in life, it is good to ask whether it will be a good place from which to go on as well as a good place to remain.

MARY CATHERINE BATESON

How will I ever be able to tell
If what I achieve in life
Ought to be called serenity—not surrender?

JUDITH VIORST

. . . for as it is impossible to have every experience, one must make do with seeds—germs of what might have been.

Virginia Woolf

A new year is a clean slate, a chance to suck in your breath, decide all is not lost and give yourself another chance.

Sarah Overstreet

Fear . . . is forward. No one is afraid of yesterday.

Renata Adler

If I had to live my life again I'd make all the same mistakes— only sooner.

Tallulah Bankhead

. . . if you must leave a place that you have lived in and loved and where all your yesterdays are buried deep —leave it any way except a slow way, leave it the fastest way you can. Never turn back and never believe that an hour you remember is a better hour because it is dead. Passed years seem safe ones, vanquished ones, while the future lives in a cloud, formidable from a distance. The cloud clears as you enter it.

BERYL MARKHAM

It is the fight itself that keeps you young.

COLETTE

Experience is a good teacher, but she sends in terrific bills.

MINNA ANTRIM

I am shedding the past. It comes off me like scales.

EDNA O'BRIEN

I have always been driven by some distant music—a battle hymn no doubt—for I have been at war from the beginning. I've never looked back before. I've never had the time and it has always seemed so dangerous. To look back is to relax one's vigil.

BETTE DAVIS

The past is not a package one can lay away.

EMILY DICKINSON

The past, with its pleasures, its rewards, its foolishness, its punishments, is there for each of us forever, and it should be.

LILLIAN HELLMAN

Remembering the past gives power to the present.

FAYE MYENNE NG

Memories are our doors of escape, our compensation.
DOROTHY DIX

Perspective means having lived in a severe state of perception for some time.
HORTENSE CALISHER

Long after an experience . . . it is seen quite differently.
DORIS LESSING

She knew what all smart women knew: Laughter made you live better and longer.
GAIL PARENT

I think laughter may be a form of courage. . . . As humans we sometimes stand tall and look into the sun and laugh, and I think we are never more brave than when we do that.

LINDA ELLERBEE

It has begun to occur to me that life is a stage I'm going through.

ELLEN GOODMAN

Often continuity is visible only in retrospect.

MARY CATHERINE BATESON

Change

To gain that worth having, it may be necessary to lose everything else.

BERNADETTE DEVLIN

Everything in life that we really accept undergoes a change. This is the thing that in the greatest is a shining light, a pure white fire; and in the humblest is a constant radiance, a quiet perpetual gleam. When we stop running away, when we really accept, that is when even tragedy succumbs to beauty.

KATHERINE MANSFIELD

Life is not an easy thing to embrace, like trying to hug an elephant. . .

DIANE WAKOSKI

Why is the measure of love loss?

JEANETTE WINTERSON

We could never learn to be brave and patient, if there were only joy in the world.

HELEN KELLER

. . . joy runs deeper than despair.

CORRIE TEN BOOM

Does one come to enjoy even the hardships that help make one the person one is? Or is it that the past becomes a legend to be remembered with laughter?

MAY SARTON

. . . often our bad moments are self-propelled. . . . And the drama is almost exclusively within our heads and hearts.

KATHLEEN TYNAN

. . . we all go around ad-libbing our lives.

NAOMI FEIGELSON CHASE

You must learn day by day, year by year, to broaden your horizons. The more things you love, the more you are interested in, the more you enjoy, the more you are indignant about—the more you have left when anything happens.

ETHEL BARRYMORE

Focusing our attention—daily and hourly—not on what is wrong, but on what we love and value, allows us to participate in the birth of a better future, ushered in by the choices we make each and every day.

CAROL PEARSON

Sometimes a life, like a house, needs renovating, the smell of new wood, new rooms in the heart, unimagined until one begins the work. One rebuilds because the structure deserves a renewing.

DORIS SCHWERIN

The key to change . . . is to let go of fear.

ROSANNE CASH

. . . being troubled, or a little neurotic anyway, is kind of what comes of being alive.

SUE MILLER

Walk away from it until you're stronger. All your problems will be there when you get back, but you'll be better able to cope.

LADY BIRD JOHNSON

The moment we find the reason behind an emotion . . . the wall we have built is breached, and the positive memories it has kept from us return, too. That's why it pays to ask those painful questions. The answers can set you free.

GLORIA STEINEM

Time

Surpassingly lovely, precious days. What is there to say except: here they are. Sifting through my fingers like sand.

Joyce Carol Oates

Before, I always lived in anticipation . . . that it was all a preparation for something else, something 'greater,' more 'genuine.' But that feeling has dropped away from me completely. I live here-and-now, this minute, this day, to the full, and the life is worth living.

Etty Hillesum

Each morning I wake up and say, "Dear Lord, I don't want anything better; just send me more of the same."
KITTY CARLISLE HART

Some things are very important and some are very unimportant. To know the difference is what we are given life to find out.
ANNA F. TREVISAN

How is it that so often . . . I get the feeling I've worked hard to learn something I already know, or knew, once.
LINDA ELLERBEE

Creating meaningful personal rituals throughout the day eliminates the dullness of routine, enriches and elevates the events of our lives and at the same time comforts us.
ALEXANDRA STODDARD

Millions long for immortality who do not know what to do with themselves on a rainy Sunday afternoon.

SUSAN ERTZ

People would have more leisure time if it weren't for all the leisure-time activities that use it up.

PEG BRACKEN

It's terrible to allow conventional habits to gain hold . . . to eat, sleep and live by clock ticks.

ZELDA FITZGERALD

As soon as life becomes bearable we stop analyzing it. . . . A tranquil day is spoiled by being examined.

GEORGE SAND

Instant gratification takes too long.

CARRIE FISHER

To many people, time is still money, yet those who offend would probably never think of stealing goods or money.

BARBARA WOODHOUSE

Time is the one thing with which all women should be miserly.

AGNES E. MEYER

There were hours in every life that needed to be obliterated, but there were also those which were very nearly sacred.

ROSEMARY SIMPSON

Never be afraid to sit awhile and think.

LORRAINE HANSBERRY

The division of one day from the next must be one of the most profound peculiarities of life on this planet. It is, on the whole, a merciful arrangement. We are not condemned to sustained flights of being, but are constantly refreshed by little holidays from ourselves.

IRIS MURDOCH

. . . Time runs
Over the edge and all exists in all.

MURIEL RUKEYSER

Experience

Every age can be enchanting, provided you live within it.
BRIGITTE BARDOT

We are all the same people as we were at three, six, ten or twenty years old. More noticeably so, perhaps, at six or seven, because we were not pretending so much then.
AGATHA CHRISTIE

Time's passage through the memory is like molten glass that can be opaque or crystallize at any given moment at will: a thousand days are melted into one conversation, one glance, one hurt, and one hurt can be shattered and sprinkled over a thousand.

GLORIA NAYLOR

Though time is immediately chafing, we owe to it the amplitude and delicacy of our interior landscapes as we age.

ANNE TRUITT

Life should be like a steady, visible light.

KATHERINE MANSFIELD

The process of maturing is an art to be learned, an effort to be sustained.

MAYRA MANNES

She had understood some time ago that nothing became real for her until she had had time to live it over again.
ELIZABETH BOWEN

Maturity: A stoic response to endless reality.
CARRIE FISHER

A cynical young person is almost the saddest sight to see, because it means that he or she has gone from knowing nothing to believing nothing.
MAYA ANGELOU

If you don't want to get old, don't mellow.
LINDA ELLERBEE

Age becomes reality when you hear someone refer to "that attractive young woman standing next to the woman in the green dress," and you find that you're the one in the green dress.

LOIS WYSE

Lives are like chairs: Some are tufted and gimped more richly, some stiff and plumped up because they sit in shadowy corners unused; some hide broken springs, clotted balls of stuffing—the secrets of years covered and re-covered by fancy fabric. Some lives are hard wooden chairs indented by years of body weight, smoothed by the touch of hands.

DORIS SCHWERIN

It is idle to pretend that the world feels as fresh when you are 60 as it does when you are 21. You have seen too much of it. . . . literature is more thrilling before critical relativity arises; the worst of wine, in the early years of one's life, is better than the best toward the end.

JAN MORRIS

Old age ain't no place for sissies.
BETTE DAVIS

What used to be old is middle-aged now, and what used to be ancient is just old.
JOYCE BROTHERS

One of the many things nobody ever tells you about middle age is that it's such a nice change from being young.
DOROTHY CANFIELD FISHER

How do you tell your mother that you feel you're getting . . . old? If I'm . . . old, then what is she?
GAIL PARENT

Old age is like a plane flying through a storm. Once you're aboard, there's nothing you can do.
GOLDA MEIR

I have to be a miracle of quiet to make the flame in my heart burn low, and on some days I am a miracle of quiet. But I cannot conceive how age and tranquility came to be synonymous.

FLORIDA SCOTT-MAXWELL

There's no doubt that old age is a journey into a foreign country, so that one is constantly being astonished by what is not possible. . . .

MAY SARTON

One keeps forgetting old age up to the very brink of the grave.

COLETTE

At our age we can get rid of a lot of superficials. Vanity for one thing. . . . We can relax in whatever is becoming and comfortable. We don't have to be "house-proud" and struggle over our possessions. . . . Many of our duties to family, to town or country, have dropped. We are freer now to do what we want. We can choose our pleasures, without guilt, be ourselves without pretense. . . .

ANNE MORROW LINDBERGH

Surely the consolation prize of age is in finding out how few things are worth worrying over, and how many things that we once desired, we don't want anymore.

Dorothy Dix

What I have always loved most in men is imperfection. I get moved by the wrinkles on the throat of a man. It makes me love him more. I think it is sad that more women don't take the chance that maybe men will be moved by seeing the chin a little less firm than it used to be, that a man will be *more* in love with his wife because he remembers who she was and sees who she is and thinks, God, isn't that lovely that this happened to her. And be moved by life telling its story there.

Liv Ullmann

One of the signs of passing youth is the birth of a sense of fellowship with other human beings as we take our place among them.

Virginia Woolf

The wisdom of those who have lived longer than I, though I never recognize it at the moment, is afterwards nearly always justified.

ANAÏS NIN

I believe the true function of age is memory. I'm recording as fast as I can.

RITA MAE BROWN

I shall not grow conservative with age.

ELIZABETH CADY STANTON

When I reached retirement age, I made up my mind that I would live this period as if my whole life was in front of me.

MINNA KEAL

Truth

. . . we carry a few grains of folly to our ounce of wisdom.

GEORGE ELIOT

Don't confuse me with the facts!

CONNIE FRANCIS

We want the facts to fit the preconceptions. When they don't, it is easier to ignore the facts than to change the preconceptions.

JESSAMYN WEST

They who see only what they wish to see in those around them are very fortunate.

MARIE BASHKIRTSEFF

. . . seeing the truth of people and events and things needed an act of the imagination, for the truth was never presented whole to one's senses at any particular moment. . .

JOANNA FIELD

There are very few human beings who receive the truth, complete and staggering, by instant illumination. Most of us acquire it fragment by fragment, on a small scale, by successive developments, cellularly, like a laborious mosaic.

ANAÏS NIN

The Truth must dazzle gradually
Or every man be blind. . . .
EMILY DICKINSON

The trouble about man is twofold. He cannot learn truths which are too complicated; he forgets truths which are too simple.
DAME REBECCA WEST

Hypothetical questions get hypothetical answers.
JOAN BAEZ

Man has no nobler function than to defend the truth.
RUTH McKENNEY

Character is the architecture of the being.
LOUISE NEVELSON

Honesty . . . makes me feel powerful in a difficult world.
CHER

Wit has truth in it; wisecracking is simply calisthenics with words.
DOROTHY PARKER

Gossip is often true. . . . But mostly, gossip is half-true. Between the two poles of whole-truth and half-truth is slung the hammock in which we all rock.
SHANA ALEXANDER

Never to lie is to have no lock on your door.
ELIZABETH BOWEN

Cynicism is an unpleasant way of saying the truth.

LILLIAN HELLMAN

Nagging is the repetition of unpalatable truths.

EDITH SUMMERSKILL

The real questions are the ones that obtrude upon your consciousness whether you like it or not, the ones that make your mind start vibrating like a jackhammer, the ones that you "come to terms with" only to discover that they are still there. The real questions refuse to be placated. They barge into your life at the times when it seems most important for them to stay away. They are the questions asked most frequently and answered most inadequately, the ones that reveal their true natures slowly, reluctantly, most often against your will.

INGRID BENGIS

Not knowing . . . was hard; knowing . . . was harder.

TONI MORRISON

What would happen if one woman told the
truth about her life?
The world would split open.

MURIEL RUKEYSER

I have to live with my own truth.
I have to live with it.
You live with your own truth.
I cannot live with it.

MARIA IRENE FORNES

Secrets

There are some secrets which scarcely admit of being disclosed even to ourselves.
JANE WEST

Nobody ever confides a secret to one person only. No one destroys all copies of a document.
RENATA ADLER

There aren't enough secrets to go round. . .
SHELAGH DELANEY

. . . truth could never be wholly contained in words. . . .
At the same moment the mouth is speaking one thing,
the heart is saying another. . . .

CATHARINE MARSHALL

Tell all the Truth but tell it Slant—
Success in Circuit lies.

EMILY DICKINSON

Isn't privacy about keeping taboos in their place?

KATE MILLETT

. . . even when we say nothing our clothes are talking
noisily to everyone who sees us, telling them who we are,
where we come from, what we like to do in bed and a
dozen other intimate things. . .

ALISON LURIE

The right to reticence seems earned only by having nothing to hide.

JILL JOHNSTON

Every one of us lives his life just once; if we are honest, to live once is enough.

GRETA GARBO

[Women] . . . are the custodians of the world's best-kept secret: Merely the private lives of one-half of humanity.

CAROLYN KIZER

The entire being of a woman is a secret which should be kept.

ISAK DINESEN

Reading

Poetry always goes straight to the marrow.
EDNA O'BRIEN

The words! I collected them in all shapes and sizes and
hung them like bangles in my mind.
HORTENSE CALISHER

151

If I feel physically as if the top of my head were taken off, I know that is poetry.

EMILY DICKINSON

Poetry, I have discovered, is always unexpected and always as faithful and honest as dreams.

ALICE WALKER

Some say life is the thing, but I prefer reading.

RUTH RENDELL

If I read a book that impresses me, I have to take myself firmly in hand before I mix with other people; otherwise they would think my mind rather queer.

ANNE FRANK

Just the knowledge that a good book is waiting one at the end of a long day makes that day happier.

KATHLEEN NORRIS

Only one hour in the normal day is more pleasurable than the hour spent in bed with a book before going to sleep, and that is the hour spent in bed with a book after being called in the morning.

ROSE MACAULAY

The pleasure of all reading is doubled when one lives with another who shares the same books.

KATHERINE MANSFIELD

What one has not experienced one will never understand in print.

ISADORA DUNCAN

The real power of books is their deep companionability. We learn from them as we learn from the deep companionability of love to know our own hearts and minds better.

JANE RULE

I love [quotations] because it is a joy to find thoughts one might have, beautifully expressed with much authority by someone recognizedly wiser than oneself.

MARLENE DIETRICH

When I was a ten-year-old bookworm and used to kiss the dust jacket pictures of authors as if they were icons, it used to amaze me that these remote people could provoke me to love.

ERICA JONG

No time is ever wasted if you have a book along as a companion.

MARIAN WRIGHT EDELMAN

Writing

Nothing has really happened until it has been recorded.
VIRGINIA WOOLF

A thing is incredible, if ever, only after it is told—
returned to the world it came out of.
EUDORA WELTY

One may lie to oneself, lie to the world, lie to God, even, but to one's pen one cannot lie.
WILLA CATHER

The impulse to write things down is a peculiarly compulsive one, inexplicable to those who do not share it, useful only accidentally, only secondarily, in the way that any compulsion tries to justify itself.
JOAN DIDION

This is my answer to the gap between ideas and action—I will write it out. In the way that is natural to me. There I will dare anything.
HORTENSE CALISHER

We rely upon poets, the philosophers, and the playwrights to articulate what most of us can feel, in joy or sorrow. They illuminate the thoughts for which we only grope; they give us the strength and balm we cannot find in ourselves. Whenever I feel my courage wavering I rush to them. They give me the wisdom of acceptance, the will and resilience to push on.

HELEN HAYES

Poets are regular people who live down the block and do simple things like wash clothes and stir soup.

NAOMI SHIHAB NYE

If everybody became a poet the world would be much better. We would all read each other.

NIKKI GIOVANNI

I'm not sure a bad person can write a good book. If art doesn't make us better, then what on earth is it for?
ALICE WALKER

As I am a poet I express what I believe, and I fight against whatever I oppose, in poetry.
JUNE JORDAN

Words are your material, and if you can use them, then fight with them and wrestle them because they are alive.
JEANETTE WINTERSON

I suppose I am a born novelist, for the things I imagine are more vital and vivid to me than the things I remember.
ELLEN GLASGOW

Writing was the soul of everything else. . . . Wanting to be a writer was wanting to be a person.

PATRICIA HAMPL

. . . the writer must hew the phantom rock.

CARSON MCCULLERS

People who happen to write novels are nervous. . . . And their nervousness is fully justified, it seems to me. I say "who happen to write novels," meaning to put it just that way, for I really think no one can *will* a novel into existence, and that deep down everyone who attempts to write one recognizes this.

DIANA CHANG

When I'm asked why Southern writers particularly have a penchant for writing about freaks, I say it's because we are still able to recognize one.

FLANNERY O'CONNOR

When you write you lay out a line of words. The line of words is a miner's pick, a woodcarver's gouge, a surgeon's probe. You wield it, and it digs a path you follow. Soon you find yourself deep in new territory. Is it a dead end, or have you located the real subject? You will know tomorrow, or this time next year. . . .

ANNIE DILLARD

Sometimes students ask, "Are you famous?", as if fame is what would make a poet happy. I prefer the idea of being invisible, travelling through the world lightly, seeing and remembering as much as I can.

NAOMI SHIHAB NYE

If I waited for perfection . . . I would never write a word.

MARGARET ATWOOD

We inherit a great responsibility as well for we must give voice to centuries not only of silent bitterness and hate but also of neighborly kindness and sustaining love.

ALICE WALKER

Although some use stories as entertainment alone, tales are, in their oldest sense, a healing art. Some are called to this healing art, and the best, to my lights, are those who have lain with the story and found all its matching parts inside themselves and at depth. . . . In the best tellers I know, the stories grow out of their lives like roots grow a tree. The stories have grown *them*, grown them into who they are.

CLARISSA PINKOLA ESTÉS

Always, both when I started and now, to me writing is a covert act.

EDNA O'BRIEN

With a pencil and paper, I could revise the world.

ALISON LURIE

163

Art

. . . everybody who is human has something to express. Try *not* expressing anything for twenty-four hours and see what happens. You will nearly burst.

BRENDA UELAND

We are artists because we are ourselves.

ANNE TRUITT

Art lives and dies in the unique heart of he who carries it, just as all feelings only live and expand in the souls of those who feel them. There is no history of art—there is the history of artists.

MARIANE WEREFKIN

. . . the artist is not there to be at one with the world, he is there to transform it.

ANAÏS NIN

For an artist there is great value in being invisible. Only when you can stop looking at yourself do you become capable of filling other bodies.

GAIL GODWIN

I think most of the people involved in any art always secretly wonder whether they are really there because they're good or there because they're lucky. If they have time to think.

KATHARINE HEPBURN

I think every work of art is an act of faith, or we wouldn't bother to do it. It is a message in a bottle, a shout in the dark. It's saying "I'm here and I believe that you are somewhere and that you will answer if necessary across time, not necessarily in my lifetime."

JEANETTE WINTERSON

To be an artist includes much; one must possess many gifts—absolute gifts—which have been acquired by one's own effort. And moreover, to succeed, the artist must possess the courageous soul . . . the brave soul. The soul that dares and defies.

KATE CHOPIN

Some of us come on earth seeing—Some of us come on earth seeing color.

LOUISE NEVELSON

How can people think that artists seek a name? A name, like a face, is something you have when you're not alone. There is no such thing as an artist: there is only the world, lit or unlit as the light allows. When the candle is burning, who looks at the wick? When the candle is out, who needs it? But the world without light is wasteland and chaos. . . .

ANNIE DILLARD

I believe that to create one's own world in any of the arts takes courage.

GEORGIA O'KEEFFE

We are stimulated to emotional response not by works that confirm our sense of the world, but by works that challenge it.

JOYCE CAROL OATES

168

Interpretation is the revenge of the intellect upon art.
SUSAN SONTAG

Art is an investigation.
TWYLA THARP

Art is a protest against death.
AUDREY FLACK

. . . nothing is so humble that it cannot be made into art.
SARI DIEVES

Imagination

. . . imagination . . . is the source of all my unhappiness
as well as of my pleasures.
ANAÏS NIN

A thinking woman sleeps with monsters.
ADRIENNE RICH

Genius, whether locked up in a cell or roaming at large, is always solitary . . .

GEORGE SAND

It takes a lot of time being a genius, you have to sit around so much doing nothing.

GERTRUDE STEIN

. . . inspiration never arrived when you were searching for it.

LISA ALTHER

Inspiration . . . comes into us slowly and quietly and all the time, though we must regularly and every day give it a little chance to start flowing, prime it with a little solitude and idleness.

BRENDA UELAND

Imagination has to do with one's awareness of the reality of other people as well as of one's own reality. Imagination is a bridge between the provincialism of the self and the great world.

PAULA FOX

All prosperity begins in the mind and is dependent only upon the full use of our creative imagination.

RUTH ROSS

. . . the key to life is imagination. If you don't have that, no matter what you have, it's meaningless. If you do have imagination . . . you can make a feast of straw.

JANE STANTON HITCHCOCK

Intuition is really nothing more than a . . . subconscious accumulation of experiences that you've had that you don't think about consciously anymore.

GERTRUDE ELION

A good idea will keep you awake during the morning, but a great idea will keep you awake during the night.

MARILYN VOS SAVANT

Original thought is like original sin: both happened before you were born to people you could not possibly have met.

FRAN LEBOWITZ

It is wonderful to be in on the creation of something, see it used, and then walk away and smile at it.
LADY BIRD JOHNSON

Creativity can be described as letting go of certainties.
GAIL SHEEHY

Imagination is the highest kite that can fly.
LAUREN BACALL

Improvisation can be either a last resort or an established way of evoking creativity. Sometimes a pattern chosen by default can become a path of preference.
MARY CATHERINE BATESON

Want is the mistress of invention.
SUSANNAH CENTILIVRE

A guilty conscience is the mother of invention.
CAROLYN WELLS

As great scientists have said and as all children know, it is above all by the imagination that we achieve perception, and compassion, and hope.
URSULA K. LE GUIN

The engineering is secondary to the vision.
CYNTHIA OZICK

Spirit

In all that I value there is a core of mystery.
MARGE PIERCY

All of us are hybrids of circumstance, habit, and genetics,
mysterious compounds who bend toward the light or the
darkness according to no plan or rule.
ROSELLEN BROWN

How beautiful what one does not understand can be!
COLETTE

I don't have all the answers—I don't even have all of the questions yet.
NANCY ZIEGENMEYER

. . . women, unlike most men, are . . . able to accept mystery, accept whatever comes to them—even if it's not logical. . .
CHER

The world is full of currents we can't lay corporeal hands on—trust, faith, gravity, magnetic fields, love. . . . They add richness to all our hours.
ERMA J. FISK

It is when you are really living in the present—working, thinking, lost, absorbed in something you care about very much, that you are living spiritually.
BRENDA UELAND

No object is mysterious. The mystery is your eye.
ELIZABETH BOWEN

Beauty and grace are performed whether or not we sense them. The least we can do is try to be there.
ANNIE DILLARD

. . . Beauty is itself an aberration, a burden, a mystery, even to itself.
DIANE ARBUS

I collect fierce beauty, and I am curator of my own collection. I do not house it in a building: most of it cannot be housed at all, and some part of it is in me, in some sense of 'in' that philosophers still quarrel about.

ALICE KOLLER

My deepest impulses are optimistic, an attitude that seems to me as spiritually necessary and proper as it is intellectually suspect.

ELLEN WILLIS

How reluctant the world is to grant complexity in us . . . how reluctant we all are. Though knowing ourselves mysterious, subtle, complex, self-contradictory.

JOYCE CAROL OATES

One must marry one's feelings to one's beliefs and ideas. That is probably the only way to achieve a measure of harmony in one's life.

ETTY HILLESUM

Truly great people emit a light that warms the hearts of those around them.

BANANA YOSHIMOTO

. . . immortality is the passing of a soul through many lives or experiences, and such as are truly lived, used, and learned, help on to the next, each growing richer, happier and higher, carrying with it only the real memories of what has gone before. . .

LOUISA MAY ALCOTT

That is happiness; to be dissolved into something complete and great.
WILLA CATHER

The first feeling was hunger for reality and sincerity, a desire for simplicity.
GEORGIA O'KEEFFE

. . . innocence is the spirit's unself-conscious state at any moment of pure devotion to any object.
ANNIE DILLARD

Walking, I learned, is a kind of prayer, the body swinging along at a steady rhythm as the legs and feet dance ever onwards and the soul is released . . .
MICHELE ROBERTS

This is a period of transition. The perfect balance between the heart and the mind, the body and the spirit, is still to be attained.

SARA TEASDALE FILSINGER

We must walk in balance on the earth—a foot in spirit and a foot in the physical.

LYNN ANDREWS

Ages coil within
The minute Circumference
Of a single Brain. . .

EMILY DICKINSON

. . . your being is full of remembered song!

BERNICE LESBIA KENYON

Index